Copyright of Quality Management for the Small Business is held by
W.G. Edwards BA. FCQI. CQP. RSC.   D. Hoyle BSc. Hon FCQI. CQP.

No part of this book may be reproduced or transmitted in any form or by any means, electronic or mechanical, including recording, or by any information storage and retrieval system, without permission from the authors.

persign@aol.com; hoyle@transition-support.com

All rights reserved

First Edition 2013

ISBN 978-1491234976

The Chartered Quality Institute holds the copyright of The Small Business Standard. It is free to download from their website www.thecqi.org

# Contents

| | |
|---|---|
| **Introduction** | 1 |
| How to use the Guide | 3 |
| | |
| **Guidance notes for implementation** | 5 |
| Customer Focus | 7 |
| Management Action | 15 |
| Processes | 21 |
| Quality is Participation | 31 |
| | |
| **Self-Assessment for managing quality** | 33 |
| How to complete the self-assessment | 35 |
| Customer Focus | 37 |
| Management Actions | 45 |
| Processes | 49 |
| Scoring | 52 |
| Creating an action plan | 55 |
| Priority action list | 56 |
| How the topics relate to the Small Business Standard | 57 |
| | |
| Appendix 1. Reading and creating flowcharts | 59 |
| Appendix 2. Where things fit in. | 62 |
| Appendix 3. How the scoring works | 65 |
| | |
| Index to the requirements in the Guidance Notes | 66 |

# Introduction

This Guide to Quality Management has been prepared to help small businesses understand and apply basic quality ideas. It is based on the requirements laid out in the Chartered Quality Institute's "Small Business Standard©". Each requirement is as simple as possible but we recognize that several may need further explanation and examples. Knowing 'how to do it' is a small part, understanding why is equally important so justification for each of the actions is also included. How rigorously you address each requirement will be dependent on the size and the nature of your business.

Several people reviewed the "Small Business Standard©" before it was published, one of them made the following comment,

*"Small Business = Small team = Pushed to their limits."*

It is this comment which has been the driver for this book. We have avoided excessive or onerous activities and unnecessary paperwork. How you implement the standard is your decision. All the examples presented are from small businesses.

## Why bother with quality?

Today's customers have choice and seek services or products with the features they want. It is no longer sufficient to compete on price alone. The present economic conditions are subjecting prices to tremendous downward pressures.

At the same time, expectations on the quality of service and product have never been so high. Customers whose expectations are not met simply don't return. Quality is not nice to have, it is essential to stay in business.

## What is a quality business?

At the heart of a quality business is a clear focus on the customer. This means understanding what they want related to the service you provide and this can only be achieved by talking to them. Simply understanding their needs is not enough, the business has to deliver. Delivery has be on time, the product or service has to be at the right quality, it has to do the job it is supposed to do and the price has to be right. This alone is not enough to retain loyal customers; whether you are dealing directly with them or in a business-to-business relationship, they have other expectations of care, which must be met. Customers measure the quality of your business by how much you care for them, not just on the products you deliver.

You need to:

- Attend to the customer's needs.
- Treat the customer with courtesy and consideration.
- Be credible in what you are offering.
- Display a friendly attitude.

Repeat business is important financially. It means your customers buy with confidence; they trust your product or service and know you will deliver. You can only gain this reputation of trust by being in control of the quality of your product or service.

The Management Actions within the business support the efforts to be Customer Focused. It is through our actions that we show others we mean what we say. Effective management actions show the direction and purpose of the business, they set the standards the company needs to achieve and determine how they will be met. They ensure that resources are available and that staff have the appropriate skills to do their tasks. At their best, they encourage staff to be involved, not only in achieving the best results but also to seek and identify potential improvements.

The final piece in the jigsaw of a quality company is its delivery process. This is how the product is made or the service delivered and the customer satisfied. Key processes are understood and described. Proper checks exist to stop work going wrong. They prevent faulty product or service being provided. People know their roles and responsibilities, and understand what to do when things go awry.

When these three aspects, Customer Focus, Management Actions and Processes work together then we can consider our company a Quality Business

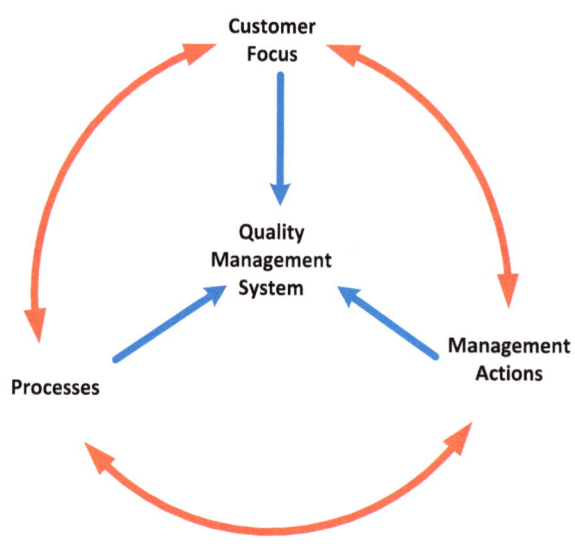

*Working together to create a Quality Management System*

# How to use the guide

The book is divided into two sections, the Guidance Notes for implementation and the Self-assessment. Read through the Guidance notes first and as you do so-

- Think about what you currently do.
- Compare this with the guidance notes.
- If they differ assess the benefits of following the practice suggested and
- Decide what you want to do.

Make notes as you go along. You can use these as the basis for any action plan. The requirements from the Chartered Quality Institute's "Small Business Standard©" are shown in *italic text.*

Then tackle the self-assessment.

## Self-assessment

There are lots of good reasons to complete a self-assessment. It provides an opportunity for you to sit back, think about your business, and consider where you can improve it.

- If you are just beginning to address the Small Business Standard it will give you a bench mark against which you can later check you progress.
- By showing what is done well and what can be improved it will help you to prioritize the areas for action.
- It can show you how well you are progressing.
- It can highlight areas of excellence in your business, where perhaps there are ideas to be shared.
- By asking others in different roles to also complete it you can discuss any differences of perception and reach a degree of understanding between those involved on where and what to improve.
- Repeated at a later date it can indicate any areas where perhaps slippage has taken place.

The pursuit of quality is a journey and the self-assessment pack will help you to chart your route of your journey which will be unique to your business.

## Create and implement your plan

From the Self-assessment you will have your priority action list. It makes sense to begin with your Quality Policy and Purpose. These will influence how you address the remainder of the requirements and tailor them to your specific needs. Now consider the remaining requirements, decide which are the most important to your business. Some will influence the whole of the business while others will exist within specific processes. If you are unsure of this then have a quick look at Appendix 2.

Do create a programme and set yourself targets for completion. It is all too easy for activities like this to drift into the car park as the daily pressures of the business must always come first.

It is important to realise that these requirements are interlinked and related in some way. A business is not a simple sequence of steps. It is a complex set of bits that interact in various ways to produce the output wanted. A consequence of this is that you may not see immediate benefits from implementing a particular requirement; it may need others to support it.

Tell your staff what you are doing and what you want to achieve. Invite them to participate, it will make the task easier and increase the sense of ownership and personal involvement.

As you progress refer to the guidance notes to see what you need to do.

It may not be necessary to finish one activity before moving on to the next. With others helping you, you can work on several at the same time.

When you have finished, review the whole package in its totality.

If in the future, you make changes to your Quality Management System refer to the guidance notes to check that changes are in the right direction.

It is beyond the scope of the guide to provide detailed information on the various legal requirements that affect your business. Compliance to the Small Business Standard does not mean that you meet all the relevant legislation. It is your responsibility to know the legislation that affects your business.

# Guidance Notes
# For
# Implementation

# Customer Focus

*Listen to customers and create a policy for satisfying their needs and expectations on delivery, price, and quality*

The quality policy exists to guide the business in achieving the results the customers want. It should act like a golden thread running through the business. The policy should direct the actions and behaviours within the business. Every business is unique so each policy has to be tailor made to suit the specific style and nature of the company. Write your policy so it is clear that everyone is responsible for quality.

The customer is the ultimate judge of a business' quality, so better Quality Policies have a clear customer focus.

Things to consider:

- the degree to which customer expectations will be met or exceeded;
- the level of customer satisfaction you want to achieve;
- the level of service you intend to supply;
- how the business intends to maintain or improve its existing level of service; and
- how staff will be supported in meeting the intent of the policy.

Of course, customers are not the only people interested in the company, and the diagram shows some of the key stakeholders.

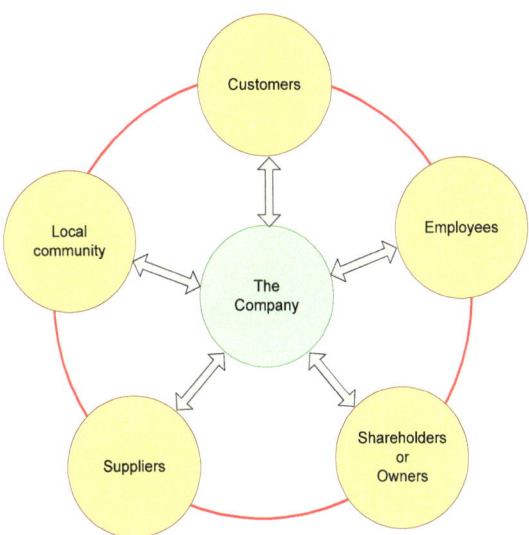

The degree of importance of each possible stakeholder will vary from company to company and it is not necessary to refer to them all. Only do so if they play an important role in reaching the business objectives or are directly affected by the business output. Your neighbours won't support you if you are polluting their neighbourhood.

In addition to the impact on the various stakeholders, you must also consider the resources required to meet the policy.

Before publishing your policy run a few simple checks:

- Ask, "Can sensible and practical lower level objectives be set from this statement?" If the answer is no then the statement needs re-visiting.

- Ask, "Can we measure the success or otherwise of this policy?" If the answer is no the policy is too vague.

- Imagine your policy is hanging on the wall of another company. Will it work for them? If so then it is probably too generic and not specific enough for your business.

- Ask others in the business, "Can you work with this, if not then what would you change?" Their answers may result in modifications.

An example Quality Policy from Navig8 (a Graphic Design Group)

We will always provide creative and unique solutions to our client's brief. Our solutions will be based on effectively achieving the desired results. We will not miss our client's deadlines and will take a proactive approach with every project ensuring the project moves forward without relying on client initiative.

Advice and support will be available during and after the project and costs will be kept to a minimum with any savings passed directly to the client. Requests from our clients will be acted on immediately.

We are committed to the continuous improvement of our products and services and this will be achieved through individual and team development and will be supported by the Small Business Standard.

*Display or otherwise communicate the policy to all staff*

The best-crafted quality policy has no value if people are unaware of it so make sure you clearly communicate it. If you have an area where you meet your customers consider displaying it for them to see.

*Accurately describe the product or service offered in any advertising material or catalogues*

It is not just what you deliver that builds your reputation. How you advertise and promote your product or service sets customer expectations. So it has a significant impact. If customers feel misled they won't return and worse they will tell others.

- Don't make any claims for your product or service that cannot be fully justified. Make sure product claims, such as CE marking, are used correctly.
- Review the proofs of any printed material carefully before releasing them to the public.
- Make sure that any images used truly represent the product or service you provide.

*Understand and agree the customer requirements with the customer before work commences*

The most expensive errors to correct are those made at the beginning and not discovered until the end. Customers can be vague about what they want. They have come to you because you are the experts. It is better to offer them something from which they will derive the most benefit not something from which you will derive the most revenue.

- Understand the use the customer wants to make of the service.
- Find out if it has to align with other activities;
- If it's a product, how will it be used? What materials are needed?
- What quality standards will apply?
- State exactly what the product or service will do.
- State exactly what it won't do.
- Depending on the size of the project, it may be necessary to write out a full specification. If you do, get the customer to agree the specification correctly defines the requirements.

*Accept only those orders where the customer requirements can be met in full*

It can be very tempting when offered a potentially large piece of business to immediately order the champagne. But be wary. Before taking on any new business check that resources are available to do the work. If the customer needs delivery on a specific date delivering a day later is not acceptable. It may result in rejection of the delivery and you'll be left holding stuff you don't want and haven't been paid for.

Completing the following checks can protect your business:

- Can delivery be made in the required time with the existing staff, equipment and facilities?
- If needed, can you increase capacity or capability in time?
- If extra people are needed, can they be trained adequately? Taking experienced people off the job to support and supervise others can have a cost. You may find that productivity and quality actually goes down at first. So don't simply think extra numbers will be sufficient;
- If machinery or special equipment is needed does it need to run longer than usual?
- Will your suppliers be able to respond to your extra demands?
- Will overtime be required? If so how will the increased cost affect your profit margin?
- Check your cash flow carefully. Extra expenditure on wages and materials may cause problems.

At Benchmark Training potential new work is subjected to their seven tests of principle.

Benchmark Training's Seven Tests of Principle

1. Do we fully understand the requirements of the opportunity?
2. Is the business opportunity consistent with the Benchmark's strategic business plan and/or direction?
3. Does the business opportunity fit within our broad capability area and with our market positioning strategy?
4. Does the Company have the willingness, potential and capability to pursue the opportunity through the application of cost-effective and available resources?
5. Is the Board satisfied that appropriate exit points exist to ensure the sustained and effective management of risk?

6. Does the opportunity provide for a reasonably sized potential market?
7. Are there any other existing factors that might influence the Board's decision?

## *Include everything that significantly influences the price in any quotation given*

No one likes surprises. When preparing a quotation do include everything that affects the price. Don't try to win the contract by omitting necessary items in an attempt to keep the cost low. The customer won't thank you and you probably won't get repeat business if it becomes necessary to increase the cost to the customer half way through the work.

If you frequently prepare complex quotations then consider producing a checklist of items so nothing is missed.

A well-constructed quotation is protection against a customer that either keeps changing the requirements or tries to get you to do more than you originally quoted for without having to pay for it.

## *Check before delivery of product or during delivery of service that it matches the original requirement*

The very last person you want identifying problems is the customer. It is embarrassing and expensive to put things right at this stage. Design the checks into how the work is delivered and consider:

- ➢ Does the identity and quantity match the paperwork? Does this align with what the customer expects?
- ➢ Has it been made correctly and the agreed quality standards met?
- ➢ Is the packaging appropriate and will it protect the product?

And for service delivery:

- ➢ Is the service being delivered in the way the customer expects?
- ➢ Are all aspects of the offered service being delivered?
- ➢ Are the required quality standards being met?
- ➢ Is it being completed in a timely manner?

*Inform customers of problems that may cause delay or changes in the product or service provided*

There will be times when things don't go quite to plan. At such times it is essential to keep the customer informed and the sooner you tell them the better. Let them know what is happening and why. Often the customer will have a solution to your problem and the last thing you want is for the customer to say, "If only you had let me know I could have rearranged but now it's going to increase costs"

Don't just let them know about the problem. Before you contact them make sure you can offer an alternative solution or a plan for putting things right.

*Manage changes in requirements to the customer's satisfaction and in a way that meets the needs of the business*

The cost of making changes increases dramatically as the order progresses through the business. You have to consider any potential change very carefully, especially in the later stages of development or production.

If the customer requests the change:

- What are the implications of the change?
    - Is a redesign necessary?
    - Can components or materials already purchased still be used?
    - Will the change affect completion and delay delivery?
- What are cost implications of the change?
    - How much will this cost to introduce/set up?
    - What is the impact on any recurring cost?
- Does the change affect the integrity of the product?

Let the customer know the implications on cost and delivery and be prepared to negotiate a new contract.

Occasionally an issue identified in-house may result in a change being requested. In this case the reason for the change must be clearly understood. If the proposed change is the result of a safety issue tell the customer as quickly as possible. Involve them in a search for a solution. Changes intended to make cost savings must be solidly based on fact.

*Protect customer property from loss or damage at all times*

For some businesses this is taken for granted, repair workshops that take in customers' property or dry cleaners that take your clothes. Often it is not so clear that you are in possession of the customer's property. This can include documents, specifications and prototypes. Make sure your people know how to identify and protect these from damage or loss. If necessary, set up a method of tracking and recording customer property.

In some instances you may hold customer data that could be covered under the Data Protection Act.

If you inadvertently damage or lose a customer's property tell the customer immediately. Work with them and reach an agreement on the necessary actions. Be open and honest for your reputation will suffer more if you attempt to cover up.

*Resolve customer complaints ensuring the problem does not recur*

Customer complaints are important. For every customer that complains there will be several who just can't be bothered, they simply take their business elsewhere. So recognise complaints are not an irritant to be got rid of but a means of understanding how you are doing in your market. When a customer complains you can be sure of one thing only, they are not happy. They may even be a little angry but it does not mean they are right. To deal with the situation effectively:

- Listen to customer carefully and try to see the situation from their point of view.
- Repeat the problem back to customer to show you have understood and are taking their comments seriously. It will show them that you care.
- Try to gain an understanding of how the problem occurred. Did the product or the service fail? Was it an expectation not met; if so was the expectation realistic? Was it a specific requirement which hasn't been met?
- Carefully consider the options available and offer the customer the option that fits the needs of your business and satisfies their concerns.
- If the level of complaints is significant then record them and analyse the records to find any underlying patterns.

It is all too easy to allocate blame when a problem arises but it is more likely that its cause lies in the processes you use.

- Has a problem like this arisen before? If so what is the pattern of events, can you repeat them?

- Talk with the people involved but make it clear that you want to understand the problem not allocate blame.
- When you are confident the problem is understood look for ways to prevent it happening again; discuss any solution with the people involved.
- Once you have implemented the solution, monitor it carefully just to make sure you haven't created a new problem.

## *Assess customer satisfaction on a regular basis*

There is no need to develop fancy questionnaires or devise complex interviews. Simply talk regularly with the customer. Make a point of calling regular customers to find out how things are going. You can ask three basic questions:

When you deal with us

- What do we do well?
- What could we do better?
- What is important to you?

What you do well you need to continue to do, what could be done better is an opportunity for the business to improve and show the customer you listen to them. If what the customer considers important is also something that could be improved then make this a priority activity.

You may consider creating a simple log of the responses so you can consider if things change over time. You can also use the log to identify any patterns that arise from different customers.

Think about what you are learning from this feedback and take actions to reinforce the positive and remove the negative.

# Management Actions

*Ensure there is a clear sense of purpose and direction*

As individuals the strongest motivator we have is our sense of personal identity. It is who we are and it drives what we do. Personal identity and culture are closely related. Creating a clear sense of purpose and direction allows people to identify with the business. It is the first step in creating the kind of culture that you want. The purpose is what your business exists for, what it does well. The direction is where you want to go, what you want to achieve. Clearly, your business plans have to align with both purpose and direction. If there is mismatch you will create uncertainty in the minds of your people. Your purpose should provide a positive image and one that is consistent with the reality of the work situation and the market place.

- Does it clarify the business you are in?
- Can the image be shared, can it be clearly communicated?
- Can it be made visible through actions and behaviours?
- Will others think it desirable?
- Will they believe it is achievable?
- Can we work together to achieve it?

Here are three examples of purpose statements:

- To design and supply road traffic management services that are trouble free for our customers.
- To provide hydraulic and pneumatic equipment maintenance services that satisfy the needs of our stakeholders and enable us to become the supplier of choice in South East Wales.
- To deliver a warranty exchange and analysis service for mobile telecommunications companies of the highest possible standard.

*Set appropriate quality standards for the product or service*

It is important for people to know whether their work has been completed correctly or not. Quality standards exist to allow them to make this judgement. They remove doubt on what is or is not acceptable. Setting a standard alone is not enough; people must also know what to do when the standard is not met. You can be confident that if there are no standards then over time the quality of the output will fall and the number of customer complaints will rise. Don't be over ambitious and don't set the standards higher than your people or machinery can achieve; doing so will increase the number of rejections and have a demoralising effect. Ultimately it is your customer who decides if your quality is good enough so set your standards against their needs and expectations.

In addition make sure your quality standards:

- don't cost more to establish and administer than the work and products to which they apply;
- are accepted as a fair basis for comparison by the people who will use them;
- cover all essential characteristics of the work and product;
- are expressed in simple and clear terms without the possibility of misinterpretation or vagueness;
- have a long enough life to provide predictability.

*Ensure that all employees have the skills, knowledge and necessary information to perform their tasks*

It is clearly the responsibility of management to ensure the overall effectiveness of the business and an important factor is that staff can perform their tasks well and right first time. It is through effective training that you can improve efficiency, improve quality and become a more successful and competitive business. There are four stages to the training activities to consider:

- Identify the need for training-
    - There is a new starter.
    - Some tasks are not being completed effectively or an individual is underperforming.
    - New tasks have been introduced into the business.
    - An individual has been transferred from one section to another.
    - A key task can only be done by one individual and you need to maintain continuity in the event of holidays or sickness.
- Decide how the training will be done-
    - Can it be done 'on the job'?
    - Does it require outside help?
- Complete the training.
- Check that the training has been effective and the necessary skills and knowledge have been acquired.

Avoid allowing someone to learn by trial and error. Productivity will be low, the number of errors will increase, the risk of accident is high and in all likelihood the individual will become very demotivated.

In addition to being properly trained people also need the right information; provide sufficient to allow the individual to finish the task at the right time and in the right place.

Keeping training records is valuable for your staff and protects the business from risk.

*Provide resources so the demand for products and services can be met*

The materials required to do any task will be dependent on the task. There is a need to strike a balance between not having materials available and carrying excessive stock. There is a cost to each of these extremes and the objective should be to carry the minimum stock necessary to prevent loss of business or production. One thing to watch for is carrying excessive stock of a material that is liable to change, once change has happened all that old stock simply represents a loss.

- What is the cost of running out of stock?
- Are there items with a long lead-time?
- What is the cost of carrying excessive stock?
- What is the cost of stock made redundant through change?
- Ensure perishable items are closely controlled and not used past the use by date.

*Provide a safe and suitable work place*

A clean and tidy workplace can be a pleasure and have a positive impact on performance. The reverse is also true; a dirty and untidy place presents potential hazards, reduced productivity and does not support good work.

It is a legal requirement, once a business is over a certain size that a health and safety risk assessment is conducted, this is a positive thing to do regardless of size.

- Identify and take actions to remove or reduce any dangerous or hazardous situations.
- Make sure that the working conditions are right for the task.
- Install machinery with adequate space around them for safe working.
- Maintain and keep machinery and equipment in a safe working condition.
- Where necessary the appropriate protective clothing must be provided.
- Insist on tidiness in the workplace. Keep workspaces and desks clear of clutter.
- Reuse, recycle or otherwise safely dispose of waste; don't let it accumulate.
- Make sure people know what to if they see a hazard, e.g. an oil spill. Encourage the idea that safety is everyone's responsibility.
- Maintain the specified conditions for materials, products and manufacturing processes that are sensitive to changes in conditions.
- Provide conditions in which employee's personal belongings are secure.

*Select specialist suppliers for their capability to meet requirements*

The components or materials you purchase have an impact on the quality of your product or service so choose suppliers with care. A problem that faces many small businesses is that they do not have the purchasing power of major companies and are often reliant on a single supplier for a particular part or service. If you purchase components or materials from a nationally recognised wholesaler there is no value in including them in this assessment.

Will the potential supplier:

- Have the capability to consistently supply at the quality standard you require?
- Have the capacity to produce the quantity you require?
- Give your order equal priority if you only buy in small quantities?
- Be flexible enough if your demand is variable?
- Deliver on time?

Try to build a relationship with the key people in the supplier's business, get them to appreciate your needs and how important their product and service is to your business.

It is not only purchased materials that can affect your customers' perception of quality. If you use contract workers to deliver your service make sure that:

- they understand your quality policy;
- they recognise that they are representing your business and behave in way that enhances the reputation of your business; and
- they fully understand the nature and content of the service being delivered.

*Monitor specialist suppliers for their performance and impact on the business*

No delivery will be correct if the supplier gets the wrong information so the first and most important step is to make sure your own purchase orders are correct and complete. It must be clear exactly what you are ordering. Be careful with repeat orders, especially if there has been an update or a change to your requirements.

On receipt of delivery there is always a need to check that the right things have been delivered and in the right quantity. This is sound commercial practice and ensures that you can check your invoices against the goods delivered.

To be confident that the performance of your key suppliers is not drifting use a mechanism that highlights any mistakes and reports back to the appropriate person.

You may find errors in:

- quantity delivered;
- timeliness of delivery;
- quality of the finished article.

If problems arise that affect your ability to provide your service then talk with the supplier. Explain the impact on your business and discuss ways of avoiding the problem in the future. If problems keep recurring, despite your efforts to solve them, then it may be necessary to find an alternative source of supply.

## Encourage employees to share their ideas for improvement

A sadly underused resource in many businesses is the employees. We just 'hire a hand' and ignore the whole individual, the whole personality. The potential is substantial and it won't cost anything to release it. Allow people to participate in the day-to-day running of the business. Ask for their advice and views on how things can be improved. Encourage them to take part in small groups to solve issues that are bothersome to them. Implement as many of the ideas as you can, or better still get the team that developed them to put them into practice. The question of reward is often raised but don't give financial rewards, they will never be adequate. Instead make sure that there is plenty of visible praise and recognition.

## Locate, understand and fulfill legal requirements that relate to the business and its product or service

Obeying the law is a social responsibility for everyone and businesses are no different. Owners and Directors are responsible for keeping the business within the law. The penalties can be severe if your business harms employees or others as a consequence of not following the law. It is in everyone's best interests to make sure that the relevant laws are followed.

It is beyond the scope of this guide to cover all possible areas and not every law will apply to every business.

Some of the main areas are:

- Health and safety at work.
- Environmental. (Disposal of waste, pollution etc.).
- Fire regulations.
- Product liability.
- Consumer protection.
- Employment legislation.
- Data protection.

- Specific legislation relating to your product or service.
- Specific legislation relating to machinery.
- Industry or sector specific legislation.

If in doubt seek expert advice.

*Conduct business reviews to confirm that:*
- *policies remain relevant to the needs of the customers and the business;*
- *any changes to regulations have been identified;*
- *quality standards are achieved;*
- *agreed ways of working have been maintained;*
- *training needs have been fulfilled;*
- *actions have been identified where there is seen to be a problem.*
- *problems do not recur;*
- *previously agreed actions have been completed.*

Once or twice a year or after a significant change in the business, take time out from the day-to-day activities to look at the bigger picture. Conducting a business review is an opportunity to involve all the senior managers and to reflect on the overall performance, what has gone well and what could be improved. It is an opportunity to share ideas.

It is sensible to conduct a review before introducing any major changes so you know where you are. When the change has been completed a second review can check the impact of the change.

It isn't necessary to hold a special meeting but this does have advantages. You can use the points above as the basis for the agenda but do allow time for open discussion on other relevant topics. Keep notes of the meeting so you can refer back to them.

# Processes

*Identify the key processes needed to produce the business' product or service. Describe how these processes work together*

A process is a set of activities that are triggered by some form of input. On completion of the activities the result will usually in turn trigger another process into action.

The key processes in the business are those that create and deliver the product or service. Recognising them and how they work together provides an important foundation for future improvements, lets people know how their work affects others and can simplify the learning activities of new starters. A shared understanding of how the business works and the bits are connected will bring consistency to management decisions and even reduce conflict between individuals.

- List the key stages in the business from order intake through to despatch of product or delivery of service. Don't delve into too much detail at this stage.
- Show the inter-connections between them. Every business is different but the examples show how you can present your efforts.
- Show your diagrams to the others and be prepared to amend or alter until you have a consensus between you. It may take several attempts before you have full agreement.

The next two diagrams show how you can show your key processes. This type of top level diagram will be different for every business so don't be tempted to simply copy them. Every business is different.

**Top level diagram showing the key processes in a training business**

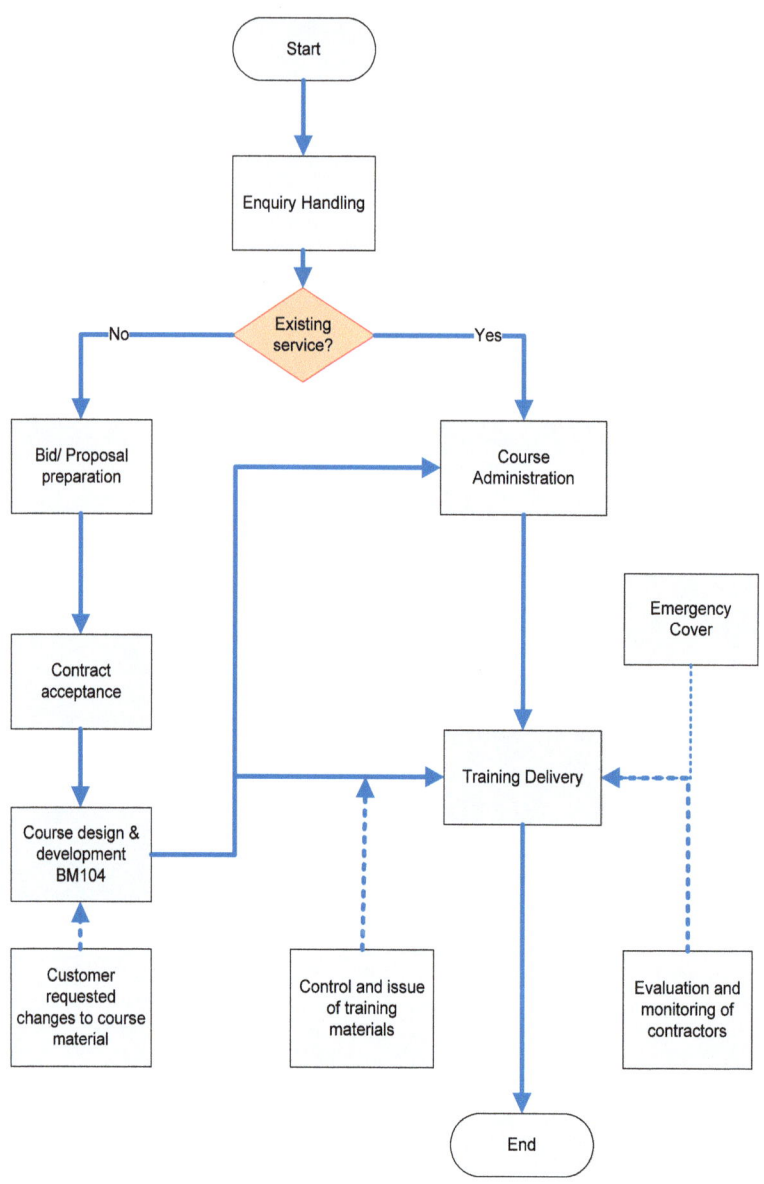

# Top level diagram showing the key processes in a small manufacturing plant

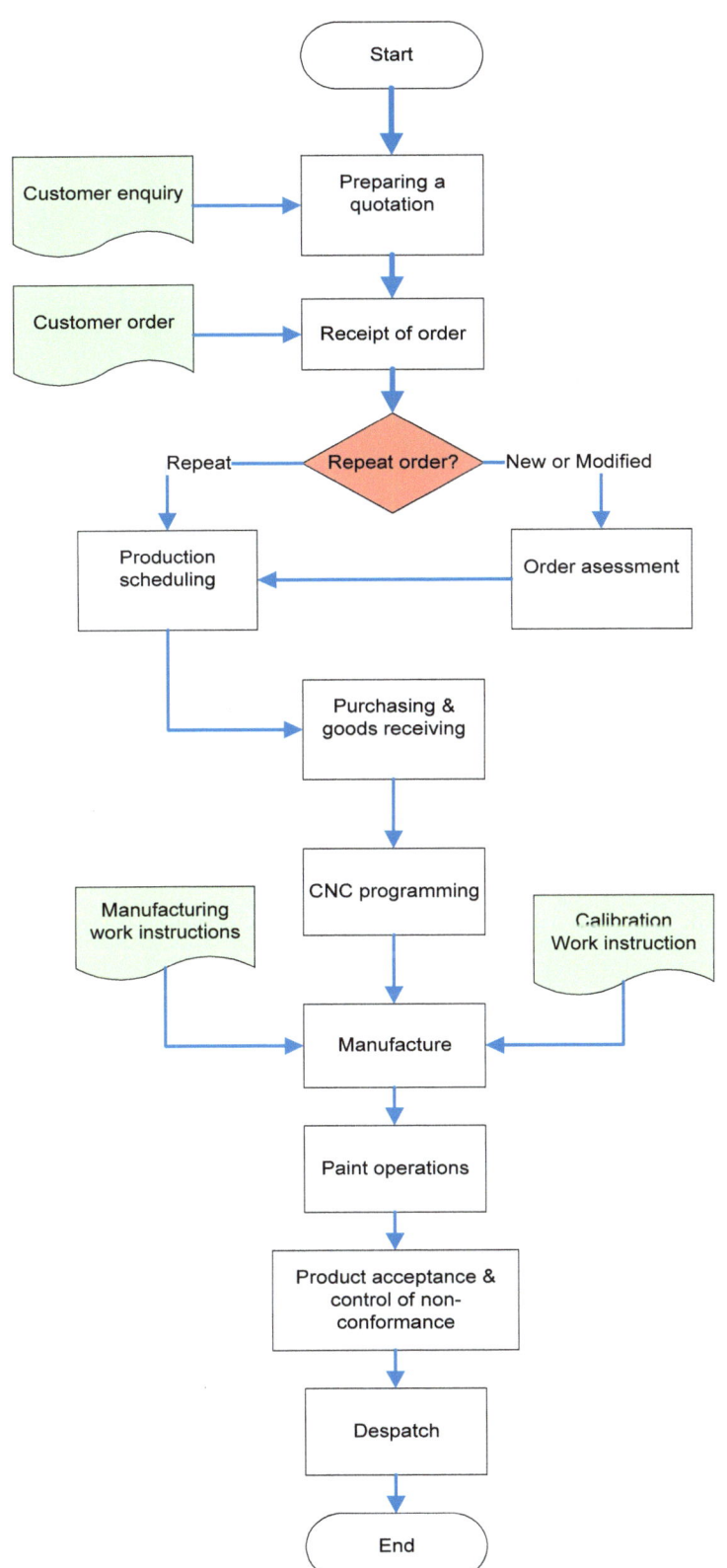

*Describe the sequence of activities within these key processes.*
*Check at regular intervals that the agreed quality standards are being maintained*

Not everyone in the business deals directly with the customer but everyone has a key role in achieving the standards the customer wants. We can think of the business as an interlinked chain with each individual adding new information or materials, which then allow the next person in the chain to do their job. Within these activities we find the necessary checks and balances needed to maintain the relevant standards are being maintained.

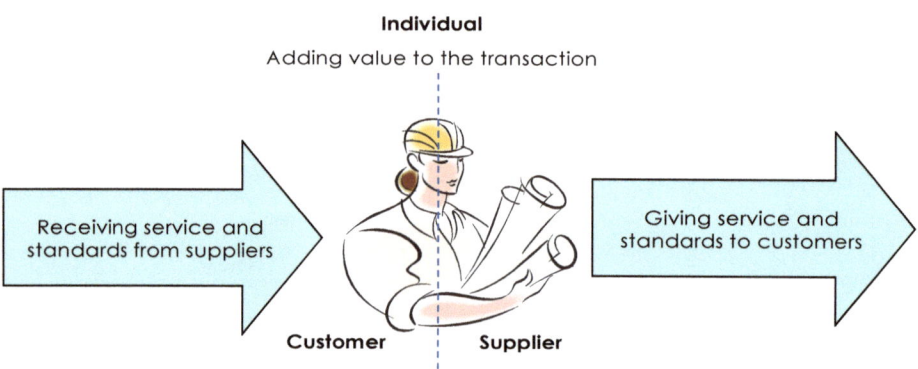

**Each individual is both an 'internal' customer and 'internal' supplier in the business chain**

We need the links in the chain to work together efficiently and to do so we need to be able to answer four main questions for each process:

- ➤ What are the needs of the next process in the set of delivery processes?
    - Who uses the output from our process?
    - Are their needs fully understood?
    - If they are not met what has to change to improve them?
- ➤ What activities need to be undertaken to achieve these needs?
    - Is the sequence of activities in a logical order?
    - Are there any duplicated activities?
    - Could any of these activities be better performed elsewhere?
- ➤ Are there checks in the process to ensure that standards are maintained?
    - Are the checks in the most effective place, close to a point where a problem may arise?
    - Do they prevent problems or just identify them? Ideally resolve immediately if any problems identified.
    - Keep any measuring equipment used at a level of accuracy appropriate to measurement being made.

- ➢ What is the input required to allow this process to operate smoothly?
    - Do we fully understand our requirements?
    - Have we discussed our needs with our internal supplier?
    - Can they meet our requirements, if not how do we have to adapt?

To answer these questions we need to have some kind of agreed description of the process. While this can be done in text, a diagram is easier to read.

This next diagram shows a detailed enquiry and proposal process. It shows the sequence of activities and how they interconnect

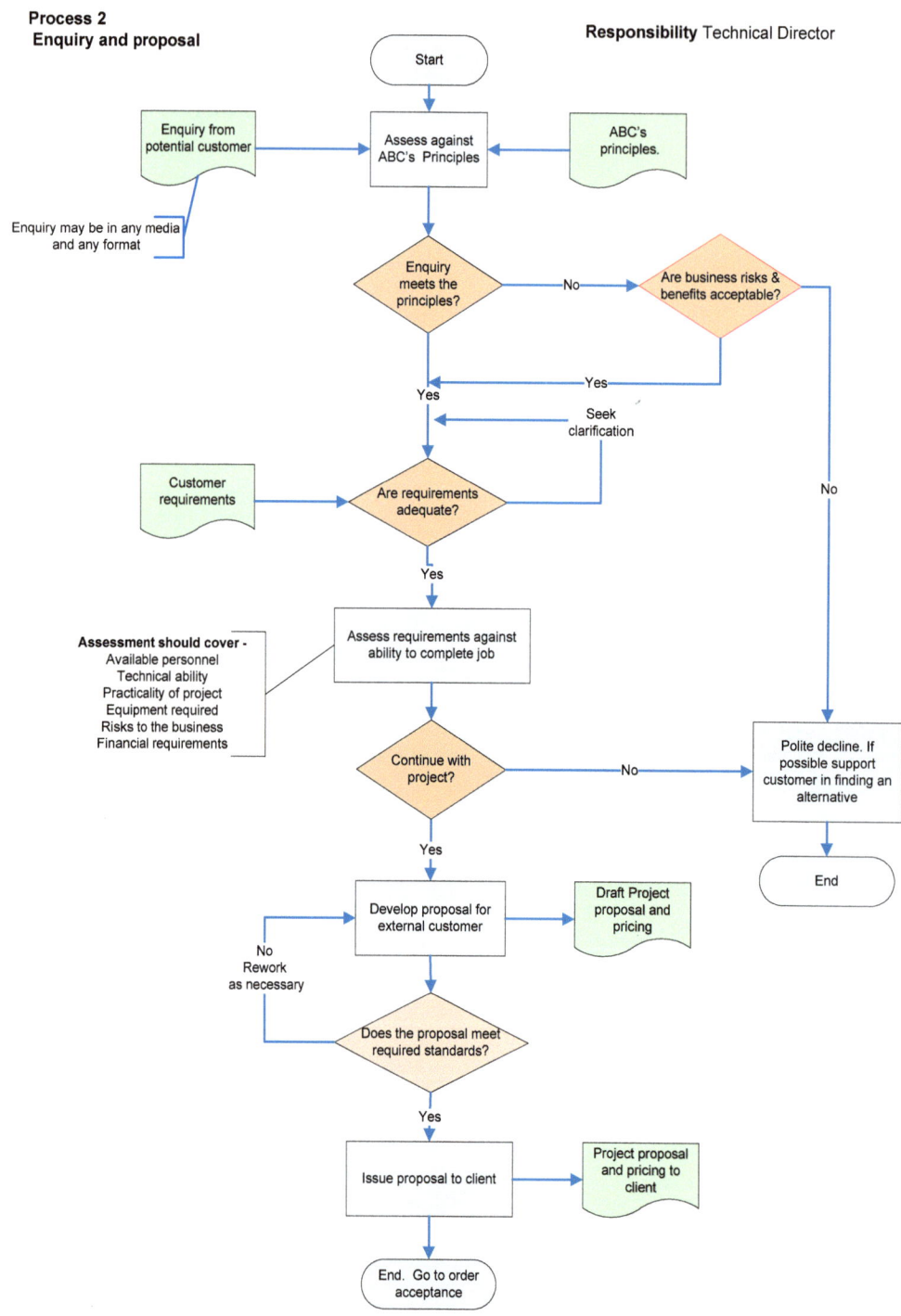

Describing your processes presents you with an opportunity to achieve several goals in the pursuit of quality.

- ➢ Involvement of personnel, leading to ownership of processes.
- ➢ The resolution of interface problems.
- ➢ The removal of activities that add no value.
- ➢ Easy to understand and check that work is being done in the agreed way.
- ➢ Development of processes, which meet the commercial needs of the business.
- ➢ Development of processes that meet the needs and expectations of your customers.

A full description of how to create flowcharts is in Appendix 1.

It is not usually necessary to describe accounting activities in detail but it is essential that those points in your processes, where information is passed to allow the correct raising of invoices, are clearly described. Clearly define who is responsible for passing accurate and timely information to accounts. Accurate and well-designed invoices enhance the businesses image.

## *Define roles and responsibilities*

Without clearly defined roles and responsibilities there is a very real risk that an important job will get missed. A situation where everyone assumes that someone else is doing it can readily arise. This can create an unpleasant atmosphere of blame and conflict. On the other side of the coin effort can unnecessarily be duplicated which again can lead to conflict and wasted resource.

If you have described your key processes it is a simple step to add the name or job title of the responsible person to the diagram. Responsibilities can only be assigned in terms of actions and decisions so before you do make someone responsible for a set of particular activities make sure that they:

- ➢ have the necessary skills and experience for the task;
- ➢ know exactly what they are required to achieve;
- ➢ have sufficient resources to finish the task;
- ➢ know what to do in the event that something goes wrong and how to put it right;
- ➢ know how to control what they are doing;
- ➢ know when they have to escalate a problem to others;
- ➢ know the limits of their authority;
- ➢ know who provides them with instructions.

It is now recognised that control activities are best carried out within the task to avoid micro-management. Avoid having all the decisions made by management as this will lead to mistrust and resentment. People are more motivated if they have a degree of self-control within their work.

*Determine what documents and records need to be kept to minimise the exposure to risk*

Documents provide us with information. Some are needed to tell people about the policies, methods of working and standards to be achieved. Others are needed to explain a proposition, a proposed course of actions or to respond to a bid or tender.

Records provide a history of what has happened and can protect the business in the event of potential litigation. They include evidence that certain actions were completed; for example, tests conducted, training given, and customer requirements understood.

It is not necessary to keep everything. Keep only those documents and records that are essential legal requirements or have a useful purpose within the business. Before deciding what to keep, address the following issues.-

- ➤ Are the documents and records legal requirements covered by the Limitations Act?
- ➤ Is there a genuine purpose for keeping the document or record?
- ➤ What risks are there if the information is not kept?
- ➤ Will resources be wasted in distributing non-essential information?
- ➤ Will we be able to keep the information correct and up to date?
- ➤ How will the information be kept safely?
- ➤ How will relevant people access to the information?
- ➤ Can sensitive information be stored securely?
- ➤ How long does the information need to be kept?

*Determine what records need to be kept enabling performance to be checked and improvements identified*

Records tell us what happened and can range from measurements taken during manufacture, test results, feedback forms from students or customers, results of reviews, time taken to process a customer order and so on. They will be different for every business but they can all serve a valuable function. They show us if performance levels are being maintained and warn us if things are beginning to go wrong. They can indicate bottle necks within the business and show us where we can make improvements. Without records it is often impossible to solve problems.

It is often necessary to compile the results into a single spread sheet before any patterns become visible.

Occasionally there may be a need to create a temporary record, especially when seeking the cause of a problem. Once the problem is solved and the temporary records have served their purpose make sure they don't become a permanent feature of the process.

- What data do we need to gather?
- Why do we need it?
- For how long do we need to collect the data?
- How long do we need to keep it?
- How will we use what we collect?

When collecting performance data make sure people understand the reason. Make it clear it is not about personal performance. If it is suspected that the data is used to judge the individual there is a very real possibility that the data will be biased and inaccurate.

## Remove the potential for error and eliminate the recurrence of problems

Errors and problems cost money, lower staff morale and destroy customer confidence. It makes sound business sense to remove any potential error and make sure that when a problem arises steps are taken to make sure it doesn't happen again. If you have followed the guidance on describing the sequence of activities within your key processes you will already have taken out many potential problems. However, there can be a tendency to drift away from the agreed method of working so it is worthwhile checking every so often that no new potential problems have been created. This is covered by the next requirement in the Small Business Standard.

When a problem arises there is a natural reaction. The situation is looked at purely in terms of the event, 'who did what, where and when'. This reactive approach produces very little real understanding and fixes you into a constant short term approach. Such descriptions are common place and the reactive approach is deeply embedded in the way we tackle problems. A better approach is to attempt to explain the situation through the pattern of behaviour. "Because of this situation, this will occur and when that happens …" Analysing patterns of behaviour moves you away from the short term event analysis by focussing on longer term trends and their implications. Don't assume the problem was caused where it appeared; a tutor can't provide excellent training if the course was not designed well and front line staff can't provide a good service if those supporting them have let them down.

*Check at regular intervals that work is consistently completed in the agreed way*

Over time the way people perform their tasks has a tendency to drift. So there is a need to check that consistency is being maintained to ensure all the effort put in to ensuring process reliability and high standards is not accidentally being undone. The frequency of these checks will depend on the complexity of the process and the risk it presents to the business if it goes wrong. These checks differ from the earlier ones in that they are done to provide confidence that the process is working in the way intended. There are three things to look at:

- Are the inputs to the process still correct?
- Does the person follow the steps described in the process description?
- Are the outputs from the process as agreed?

When the results differ from the agreed way don't automatically assume this is wrong. It may represent an improvement and an activity that added no value has been removed. However do make sure that critical checks have not been taken out.

*Manage changes to the processes in a controlled manner*

No business stands still. Improvements are found, new activities created and new people bring new ideas. All of these things bring about change in the way work is done. Do keep track of these changes; if you don't then there is the very real risk of your documented set of processes no longer reflecting the reality of the business. Sooner or later someone will attempt to complete a task the wrong way and the results won't be what the business wants.

When a change is proposed answer the following questions:

- Does the change increase or decrease efficiency?
- Does it add a layer of unwanted documentation or records?
- Does it remove a layer of documentation, if so is the documentation needed?
- Does it remove a critical check in the process?
- Does it add an unwanted check or a necessary check?
- Does it transfer work to another area, if so where is the best place for this work to be done?
- Does the change fulfil the business needs?
- Does it support the customer?

If you are satisfied that the change is an improvement update your process description and then make sure that everyone is aware of the change and that it is correctly implemented.

If it was a major change then monitor it carefully and watch for unexpected consequences especially in areas you think may be unaffected.

## Quality is Participation

The success of a business is built on its reputation. A poor reputation can take a long time to change and reputation, whether good or bad, will spread quickly.

The nature of your business will influence what creates your reputation. For each type of business the customer will require different things but one thing is always there, quality.

Quality is strategically important; it provides the competitive edge over the competition. To gain the maximum benefit quality should be a passion and everyone in the business needs to be involved in its pursuit. The ultimate judge of your product or service quality is, of course, the customer. Does it meet their needs and expectations? This is not achievable through inspection but through first understanding what the needs and expectations are and then having the right processes and resources in place. It is no longer appropriate to ask, "Have we met their needs and expectations?" Rather, "Do we have the ability to meet their needs and expectations?"

Your business reputation is only as good as the weakest link in your delivery processes. It is necessary to ensure that the needs of each internal customer, the links in the chain, are also met. Service personnel need good teamwork and communications to do their job well while in manufacturing the right tools and materials are necessary. You cannot achieve a quality company through the efftorts of one person or a small group. It needs the active participation of everyone in the business. Quality is everyone's responsibility, quality is participation. If you have implemented the requirements of the Small Business Standard with the involvement of your staff then you truly have begun the Quality Journey.

# Self-Assessment
# For
# Managing Quality

# How to complete the Self-Assessment

We have created topic statements for the requirements found in the Small Business Standard. Sometimes the topic is just about a single requirement, in others you will find two or more requirements combined. The topics remain grouped under the headings of Customer Focus, Management Actions, and Processes.

Each topic has five different scenarios, each representing a different degree of maturity, with low maturity at the bottom, and high maturity at the top of the ladder.

By choosing to write possible scenarios we realise that we cannot describe every possible situation. There will be a degree of overlap and it remains up to you to select the scenario that you think best fits your current situation. Alongside is the scoring ladder. You can place your score high or low over your chosen scenario. If you have nothing in place then you are at the bottom of the ladder.

In the example below we have three imaginary scores:
- Score A represents a situation where scenario 2 is almost completely met but the business has not yet moved into scenario 3.
- Score B represents a situation where scenario 3 is complete but the business has not moved into scenario 4.
- Score C represents a situation where the business is half way through scenario 4.

(Note you can only have one scoring point for each topic)

When you have completed your assessment you can then calculate your performance scores by using the scoring scale on page 52. This is not a straight line, and the further you progress in terms of maturity the higher the score. This reflects the impact of quality activities within the business. We show how this works in Appendix 3.

# Customer Focus
## Topic 1. How we direct attention to quality

Our policy is customer focused. We use it to guide our actions and decisions. We regularly review it for relevance and effectiveness.

Our policy is customer focused most people are aware of it. We use it to guide our actions and decisions.

Our policy is customer focused and displayed for all to read.

We have a policy but few people are aware of it.

Everyone does his or her best but we don't have a quality policy.

## Topic 2. How we bring in business

Our advertising material is up to date, accurate, and legal. We base our quotations and pricings on fact and a full understanding of customer requirements. We accept orders only when we know we have the ability to complete them. We provide accurate delivery dates. We constantly monitor our performance.

We regularly check and update all of our advertising material. We discuss and agree the requirements with the customer and prepare our quotations based on this agreement. We plan our workload and accept orders on the basis of agreed requirements. We provide delivery dates based on what we believe we can achieve.

We regularly check and update most of our advertising material. We sometimes agree the requirements with the customer and prepare any quotation based on this. We do not concern ourselves with resource requirements until the order has been placed.

Some advertising material is controlled but we have not checked it for some time.
We base quotations and pricing on experience and we include a margin for error in case we have underestimated. We accept work on the basis that we understand and can meet the customer's requirement.

We do not check our advertising material before release. We base our quotations and pricing on experience. We negotiate later if we have missed anything significant.
We simply accept orders as they arrive.

## Topic 3. How we care for customer property

We treat all customer property with care and report any loss or damage immediately to the customer. We keep it secure when we are waiting for disposal instructions from the customer. We check regularly that proper precautions are being taken.

Relevant staff know how to handle customer property, identify it and report any loss or damage to the customer.

We identify customer property when we receive it and sometimes note its intended use.

We pass customer property to the individual who needs it. It becomes their responsibility.

We don't take any special precautions with customer property and have been known to lose things sometimes.

## Topic 4A. How we stop mistakes reaching the customer (Only complete this if you deliver a product)

In addition to a final check we check at relevant stages of production to ensure that quality standards are being maintained. Prior to despatch we check for errors in the paperwork and packaging. We monitor for accuracy and consistency.

We have quality standard checks embedded in most of our processes. We only make final checks on major orders.

We check the progress of major orders and make occasional checks on lesser ones. Our packing and despatch people know what to look for.

We don't often make mistakes but our customers tell us when we do. We try to correct the situation promptly.

We have no formal way to catch errors before delivery.

## Topic 4B. How we ensure we deliver a service that meets the customer requirements (Only complete this if you provide a service)

In addition to the initial training all staff are given regular refresher courses. We monitor the delivery of the service and provide immediate refresher training if necessary. We have complete contingency plans to ensure no customer service date is missed.

In addition to the initial training all staff are given regular refresher courses. We sometimes monitor the delivery of the service. We provide additional cover when we can.

All our staff are given initial training in how to provide the service we offer.
If for any reason staff are not available on the planned date we contact the customer to rearrange another.

We rely on the experience of our people. They pass their know-how on to any new staff.
If for any reason staff are not available on the planned date we contact the customer to rearrange another

We rely on the experience of our people. They learn on the job.
If for any reason staff are not available on the planned date we contact the customer to rearrange another

## Topic 5. How we react when things don't go to plan

We have close relationships with our customers and inform them immediately there is a risk to delivery or quality. We discuss the options available with them and arrive at an agreed solution.

If we think there is likely to be a problem not of our making we will warn our customers of the risk. We advise them of the solution we are willing to offer.

In most cases we tell the customer when we know that delivery or quality will be affected. We advise them of the solution we are willing to offer.

In some cases we tell the customer about the situation but only if we have a possible solution.

We tend to try and fix the problem and hope the customer doesn't notice.

## Topic 6. How we manage changes to the customer's requirement

We process any requested change to make sure we understand the effect on quality, delivery, and cost. We discuss the implications with the customer and if the customer agrees we will then implement the change. We check that these activities work as intended.

We control change carefully and consider all customer requests. We assess the cost, delivery and quality implications but we don't have a formal method for this. We only implement change when the customer accepts the cost, delivery, and quality implications

We carefully consider change requests and check to see if it is possible. We inform the customer if the change is not possible and of the cost implications if it is.

We generally implement customer requested changes if it is not too late. We do not assess any cost implications though we may tell the customer if it will result in a delay.

We resist change especially if it undoes work already completed. If the customer insists we will implement and add any additional costs to the final invoice.

## Topic 7. How we learn how well we are doing

We are concerned over every criticism however minor it may seem. We take action to remove any repeating patterns. We monitor customer perceptions all the time and in a structured way. We take action to reinforce positive feedback and to remove the source of negative feedback.

We find an appropriate solution to all formal complaints and investigate the cause, taking action to ensure it does not recur. We frequently ask about customer's perceptions using a structured approach but we take few actions.

We attempt to find the cause all serious complaints and find a solution which is appropriate. We sometimes ask our customers about their perceptions but this not structured and there are few follow up actions.

We sometimes look at why a serious complaint occurred, especially if it has cost the business a lot of money. We rarely ask customers about their perception of our service or product and we take no follow up actions.

Complaints are seen as an irritating factor of life. We do not discuss customer's perceptions of our business with our customers.

# Management actions
## Topic 8. How we establish direction

We have a clear sense of purpose and direction that drives our business plans. Our staff are fully involved in the search for improvements and the maintenance of our quality standards. We regularly check for legislation changes and review the relevance of our purpose and direction.

We have a clear sense of purpose which we have communicated to all staff. We understand and meet all our legal requirements. Quality standards exist for our end product or service and for all key stages of development and production. A significant number of our staff are involved in improvement activities.

We have prepared a purpose statement and it is consistent with our plans. Not everyone is aware of it. We know and meet our legal requirements but we haven't checked for changes. Quality standards exist for our end product or service. Some of our staff are involved in problem solving.

We make some effort to drive the business and informal plans exist. We believe that we meet the regulatory requirements. Informal quality standards exist. Staff are not involved in the search for improvements or the resolution of problems.

The business is purely market driven. There is no sense of direction and plans are financial only. Regulatory and sector requirements have not been identified. We do not have recognized quality standards.

## Topic 9. How we provide resources and skills

We provide training to staff and management in accordance with the training plan. We have accurate training records and only allocate tasks to people trained to do the task. We plan our equipment maintenance and resource requirements. The work place is safe and suitable. We monitor our performance.

All our staff have training plans that align with our business goals. We provide resources when required. The work place is safe and suitable.

We are developing training plans and some training records exist but may not be up to date. We make H&S checks at planned intervals and all actions completed. Our workspace is structured and we maintain all key equipment.

We provide ad-hoc training but we do not plan this. We sometimes expect staff to do work for which they are inadequately trained. H&S checks made but with no follow up actions. We prepare our resources as and when we need them

Training is seen as a business cost. No health and safety checks have been conducted. Workspaces are untidy. Equipment is repaired when it breaks down. Storage space is inadequate.

## Topic 10.  How we select and monitor suppliers

Suppliers categorized on risk to the business. We have good relationships with key suppliers. When problems occur we discuss potential solutions with the supplier. There is a clear focus on quality of supply. We review both our own performance and that of suppliers at regular intervals.

Some key suppliers identified and performance monitored. Critical purchase orders are checked for accuracy and completeness.

Key suppliers not identified. Some suppliers selected on the basis of suitability and capability. We conduct little or no supplier monitoring. We use purchase orders but do not check if they are correct before release.

We select on price and change supplier when they let us down. We have an informal process for identifying purchase requirements and placing orders.

There is no supplier evaluation or selection process. We are not clear about our purchase requirements. We tend to focus on ease of supply rather than consideration of quality.

## Topic 11. How we review and assess how well we are doing

Reviews are based on existing policies, customer feedback and performance records. We implement any Improvement actions identified and check the results for effectiveness.

Reviews regularly conducted but not always based on factual evidence. Informal improvements made and the results of change informally checked.

Infrequent reviews with evidence of resulting actions. Some informal improvements initiated but with little or no follow up.

We conduct occasional informal reviews, but generate few resulting actions.

No reviews are undertaken; the business is driven by cash flow only.

# Processes
## Topic 12 How we define our processes

All processes are described. Necessary quality standard check points are clear. The quality checks are well defined. Roles and responsibilities are unambiguous. We regularly check that the process descriptions remain accurate.

We have completed 75% of our process descriptions. All points where quality standard checks are made are identified. We have clear roles and responsibilities defined for each process.

We understand how our processes work together and are starting to describe the sequence of activities within each process.

Ad-hoc descriptions of some activities exist. They are kept on individual computers.

We have little or no understanding of our business processes

## Topic 13. How we monitor and improve our processes

We check all our processes regularly and remove the cause of problems found. We base the frequency of the checks on the risk to the customer and the business. We only implement changes that are beneficial to the company. We regularly review the effectiveness of these arrangements.

We have initiated a programme of checking to ensure work is being done in a consistent way. We remove any potential for error and improvements identified are quickly implemented.

We check some of our main processes from time to time. We do not manage change and allow people to alter their process if they feel it is an improvement.

If there is a problem we will check the area where we think the fault occurred.

We do not carry out any checks on our processes.

## Topic 14. How we capture documents and data

Good records are kept and are readily retrievable for all areas of the business. Records relating to performance are constantly reviewed and patterns assessed in our business review. Customer records are current. We regularly check the effectiveness of our arrangements.

The purpose of each document and record is known. Relevant people have easy access to them and minimum storage time is known. Responsibility for safe storage is clear.

We have identified which records and documents we need to protect the company from risk and those records which inform us of how well we are doing. Access can be difficult.

We keep some records. They are difficult to access and it is not clear who is responsible for their safe storage or how long we should keep them.

No meaningful records are available to provide the basis of assessing business success or reduce any risk to the business.

# Scoring

Step 1. Complete your assessment by using the scoring ladder opposite to score each topic statement. If you placed your mark between two numbered points simply estimate its value. Write the score in the Self-assessed column on the next page.

Step 2. Multiply the self-assessed score by the multiplier then total these weighted scores to give you a total weighted score for each section.

| |
|---|
| 100 |
| 90 |
| 82 |
| 72 |
| 65 |
| 56 |
| 50 |
| 42 |
| 36 |
| 30 |
| 26 |
| 20 |
| 16 |
| 12 |
| 9 |
| 6 |
| 4 |
| 2 |
| 1 |
| 0.5 |
| 0 |

## Self-Assessed Scoring

| Topic Statement | Self-assessed Score | Multiplier | Weighted score |
|---|---|---|---|
| **Customer Focus** | | | |
| Topic Statement 1 | | X 2 | |
| Topic Statement 2 | | X 4 | |
| Topic Statement 3 | | X 1 | |
| Topic Statement 4A | | X 1 | |
| Topic Statement 4B | | X 1 | |
| Topic Statement 5 | | X 1 | |
| Topic Statement 6 | | X 1 | |
| Topic Statement 7 | | X 2 | |
| **Total weighted score for Customer focus** | | | |
| **Management Actions** | | | |
| Topic Statement 8 | | X 4 | |
| Topic Statement 9 | | X 3 | |
| Topic Statement 10 | | X 2 | |
| Topic Statement 11 | | X 1 | |
| **Total weighted score for Mgt. actions** | | | |
| **Processes** | | | |
| Topic Statement 9 | | X 5 | |
| Topic Statement 10 | | X 3 | |
| Topic Statement 11 | | X 2 | |
| **Total weighted score for Processes** | | | |
| **Total weighted score (all 3 sections)** | | | |

You can now calculate the performance scores for each section.

## Customer Focus Performance Rating

= total weighted customer focus score/12 =    ..........
(Note: If you completed both 4A and 4B you will need to divide by 13)

## Management Actions Performance Rating

= total weighted mgt. action score/10 =    ..........

## Process Performance Rating

= Total weighted process score/10 =    ..........

## Business Performance Rating

= Total weighted score/32 =    ..........
(Note: If you completed both 4A and 4B you will need to divide by 33)

# Creating an Action Plan

**Business Performance Rating**

| Score | Status | Comment |
|-------|--------|---------|
| 0-15 | Very weak | Identification of actions required |
| 16 - 25 | Weak | Actions identified need to be pursued |
| 26 - 40 | Recognition | Continue with developing and implementing the actions |
| 40 - 50 | Positive indications | You are on your way to creating a viable quality management system |
| 51 - 65 | Good | You have a reasonably well developed Quality Management System |
| 66 - 80 | Very good | There is still room for improvement |
| 81 - 100 | Excellent | There may be improvement possible but it will be difficult to identify |

Whether you've not started to implement the small business standard or have already begun the first and obvious thing to do is prioritize in terms of the scores. As a general guide we would recommend that you tackled each area in this order:-

### 1. Processes
Without adequate processes you cannot easily decide what kind of management support you should provide. Nor can you guarantee to deliver the kind of customer focus you require if the processes are not fully understood.

### 2. Management Actions
With the processes under control you can direct your efforts to the management actions.

### 3. Customer Focus
With processes understood and management support being given in the right way you can finally turn your attention to the customer.

These are just guidelines; you do not have to follow them. An alternative approach is to consider the low scoring areas and ask yourself "What damage to the business can this have in terms of cost and reputation". You can then prioritize on the basis of risk and score and complete the priority action list.

# Priority Action list

| Priority | Topic Statement | Comments |
|---|---|---|
| 1 | | |
| 2 | | |
| 3 | | |
| 4 | | |
| 5 | | |
| 6 | | |
| 7 | | |
| 8 | | |
| 9 | | |
| 10 | | |
| 11 | | |
| 12 | | |
| 13 | | |
| 14 | | |

On the next page you can see how the topics relate to the Small Business Standard.
If you need help or guidance on what to do then refer back to the Guidance Notes.

# How the topics relate to Small Business Standard

| Topic Statement | Small Business Standard Requirements |
|---|---|
| 1. How we direct attention to quality | Listen to customers and create a policy for satisfying their needs on delivery, price, and quality.<br>Display or otherwise communicate the policy to all staff. |
| 2. How we bring in the business. | Accurately describe the product or service offered in any advertising material or catalogues.<br>Understand and agree the customer requirements before work commences.<br>Accept only those orders where the customer requirements can be met in full.<br>Include everything that significantly the price in any quotation given. |
| 3. How we care for customer property. | Protect customer property from loss or damage at all times. |
| 4A. How we stop mistakes reaching the customer. | Check before delivery of product or during delivery of service that it matches the original requirements. |
| 4B. How we ensure we deliver a service that meets the customer requirements. | Check before delivery of product or during delivery of service that it matches the original requirements. |
| 5. How we react when things don't go to plan. | Inform customers of problems that may cause delay or change in the service or product ordered. |
| 6. How we manage changes to the customer requirements. | Manage changes in requirements to the customer's satisfaction and in a way that meet the needs of the business. |
| 7. How we learn how well we are doing. | Resolve customer complaints ensuring the problem does not recur.<br>Assess customer satisfaction on a regular basis. |
| 8. How we establish direction. | Ensure there is a clear sense of purpose and direction.<br>Set appropriate quality standards for the product or service.<br>Encourage employees to share their ideas for improvement.<br>Locate, understand and fulfil legal requirements that relate to the business and its product or service. |

| | |
|---|---|
| 9. How we provide resources and skills. | Ensure that all employees have the skills, knowledge and necessary information to perform their tasks. Provide resources so that the demand for product and services can be met. Provide a safe and suitable workplace. |
| 10. How we select and monitor suppliers. | Select specialist suppliers for their capability to meet requirements. Monitor specialist suppliers for their performance and impact on the businesses' product or service. |
| 11. How we review and assess how well we are doing. | Conduct business reviews. |
| 12. How we define our processes. | Identify the key processes needed to produce the businesses' product or service. Describe how these processes work together. Describe the sequence of activities within these key processes. Define roles and responsibilities. Check at regular intervals that agreed quality standards are being maintained. |
| 13. How we monitor and improve our processes. | Check at regular intervals that work is consistently completed in the described way. Remove the potential for error and eliminate the recurrence of problems. Manage changes to the processes in a controlled way. |
| 14. How we capture documents and data. | Determine what documents and records need to be kept to minimise exposure to risk. Determine what records need to be kept enabling performance to be checked and improvements identified. |

.

# Appendix 1 - Reading and creating flowcharts

The flowcharts used in this guide go under the splendid name of 'activity-sequence' diagrams. This simply means that they show the sequence of activities within the process. A very limited number of symbols are used.

**Symbols used and their meanings.**

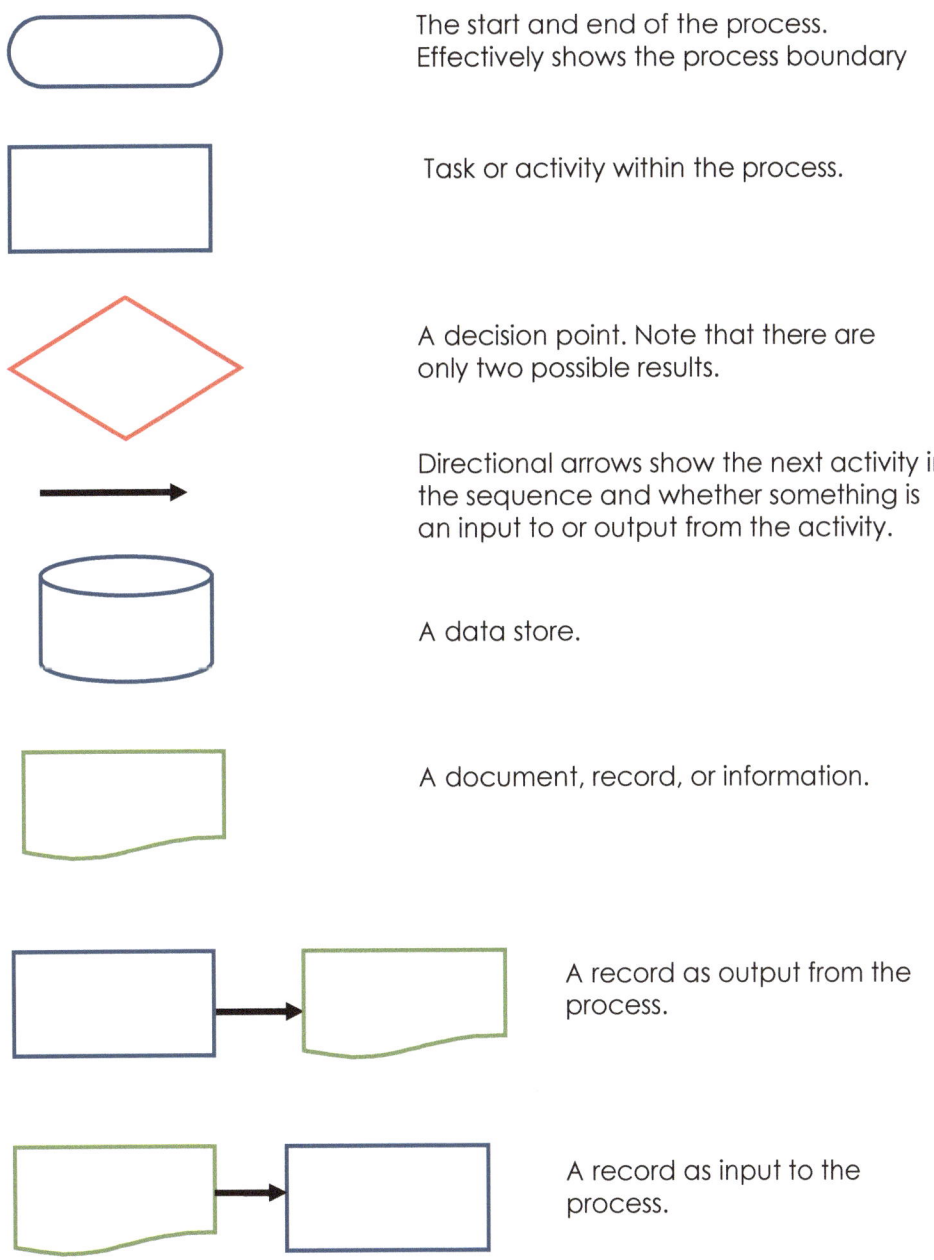

There is not one 'best approach' to creating a flow diagram but these guidelines will help:

- Agree the flow chart protocol before you start. Make sure everyone understands the meaning of the symbols used, and keep the number of symbols to a minimum.

- Identify the process owner, the person who has the authority to modify the process and ensures that it is completed.

- Involve the process users in the development of the process. These are the people who carry out the task and may or may not be the same as the Process Owner.

- Clearly define where the process begins and ends and identify the necessary inputs and outputs.

- Produce the diagram for an experienced user. Avoid too much detail and remember you are not writing a training manual.

- A detailed work instruction supporting the diagram may be necessary when:

    - It is essential that certain precautions are taken for health and safety reasons.

    - The sequence of actions is critical to the result.

    - An activity is done infrequently.

- Create a simple work instruction if an action is repeated in more than one process.

Documents in regular use only need the detail not covered by training. You have to strike a balance between training and work instruction content.

**Developing a process flow diagram** **Responsibility** ***Job Title***

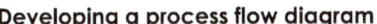

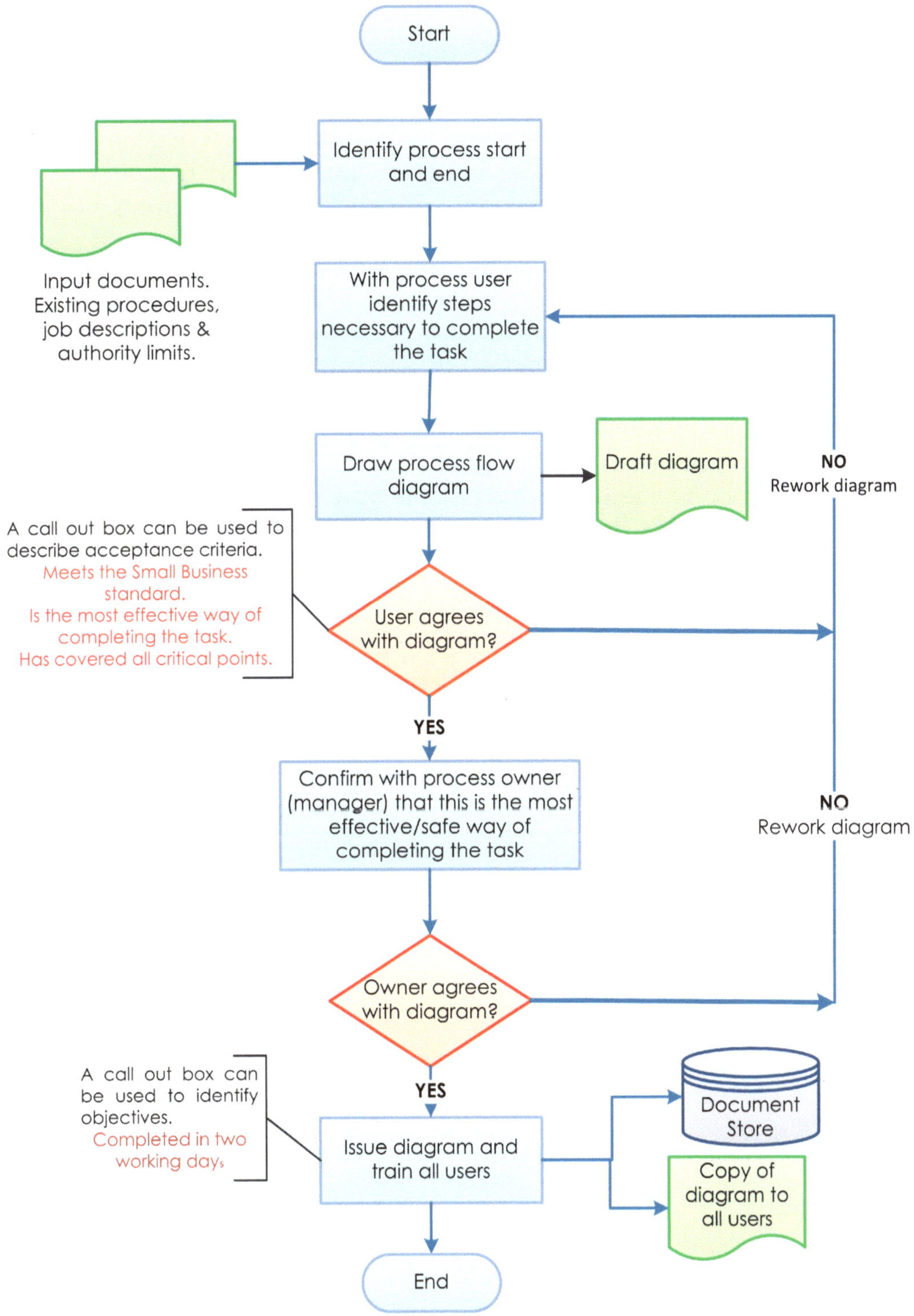

# Appendix 2 - Where things fit in

The Small Business Standard groups the requirements into three focus areas. These emphasize the importance of Customer Focus, Management Actions and Processes. In the real world things are not so tidy.

The following subdivisions are here to simply show where things fit and the general intention behind them. It is just another way of looking and thinking about the business. When you describe your processes these are the likely locations.

- ➢ Shaping requirements, they guide, direct and shape the business. They are amongst the first requirements you should consider.
- ➢ Specific requirements are found within the activities of a specific process. They relate to the process and are generally not found elsewhere.
- ➢ General requirements, these are found in all processes.
- ➢ Business Support requirements, these keep the whole business on track. They prevent the business from drifting.
- ➢ Process Support, these keep the processes on track and focus on the activities within the delivery processes.

**Shaping Requirements**

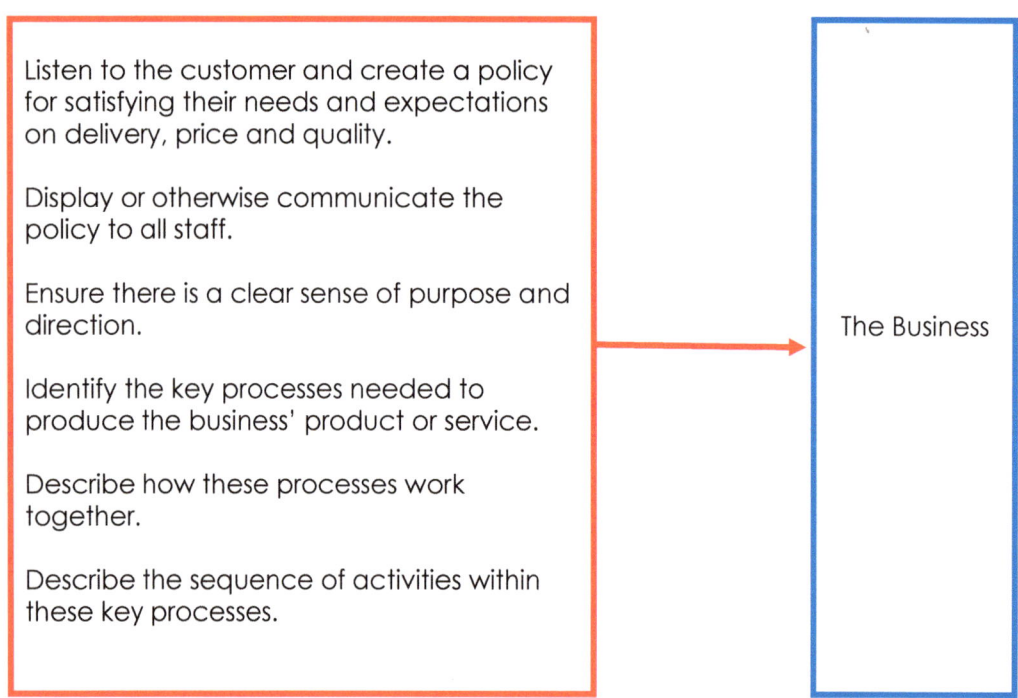

**Specific Requirements and where their application is likely to be found**

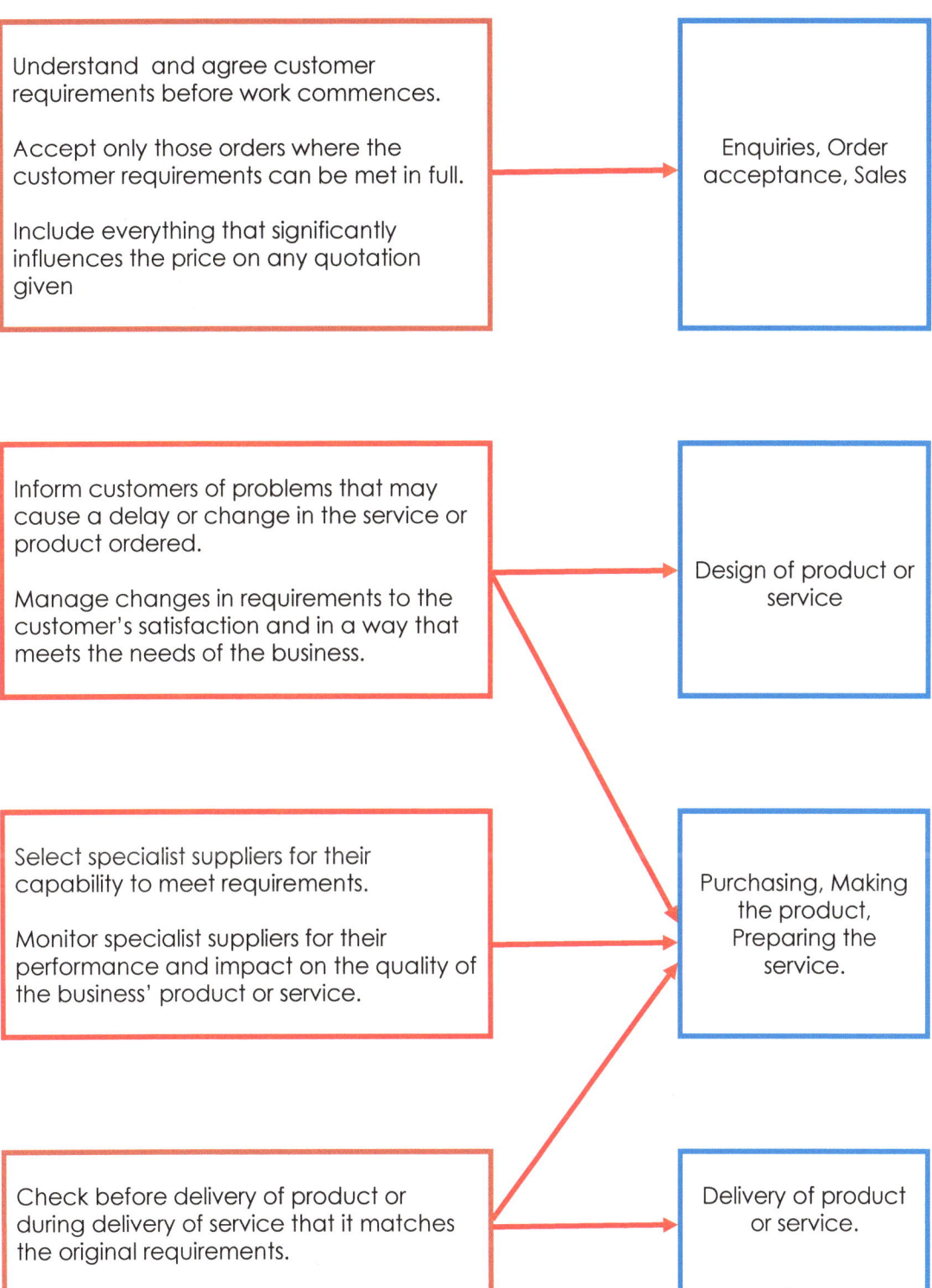

**General Requirements**

Set appropriate quality standards for the product or service.

Check at regular intervals that the agreed quality standards are being met.

Define roles and responsibilities.

Determine what documents and records need to be kept to minimize exposure to risk.

Determine what records need to be kept enabling performance to be checked and improvements identified.

Protect customer property from loss at all times.

**Business Support Requirements**

Accurately describe the product or service offered in any advertising materials or catalogues.

Resolve customer complaints ensuring the problem does not recur.

Assess customer satisfaction on a regular basis.

Ensure that all employees have the skills, knowledge and necessary information to perform their tasks.

Provide resources so the demand for products and services can be met.

Provide a safe and suitable work place.

Encourage employees to share their ideas for improvement.

Locate, understand and fulfill legal requirements that relate to the business and its product or service.

Conduct business reviews.

**Process Support Requirements**

Remove the potential for error and eliminate the recurrence of problems.

Check at regular intervals that work is conducted in the described way.

Manage changes to the processes in a controlled way.

---

Enquiries

Order acceptance

Sales

Design of product or service

Purchasing

Making the product

Preparing the Service

Delivery of product or service

# Appendix 3. How the scoring works

Quality grows, but it doesn't do so in a simple way. It is not a straight line growth. The score reflects this and a business that has just commenced their quality journey just gets a score of 25. Once this stage has passed the score increase rapidly. You get few points if the business is still in the first two scenario positions.

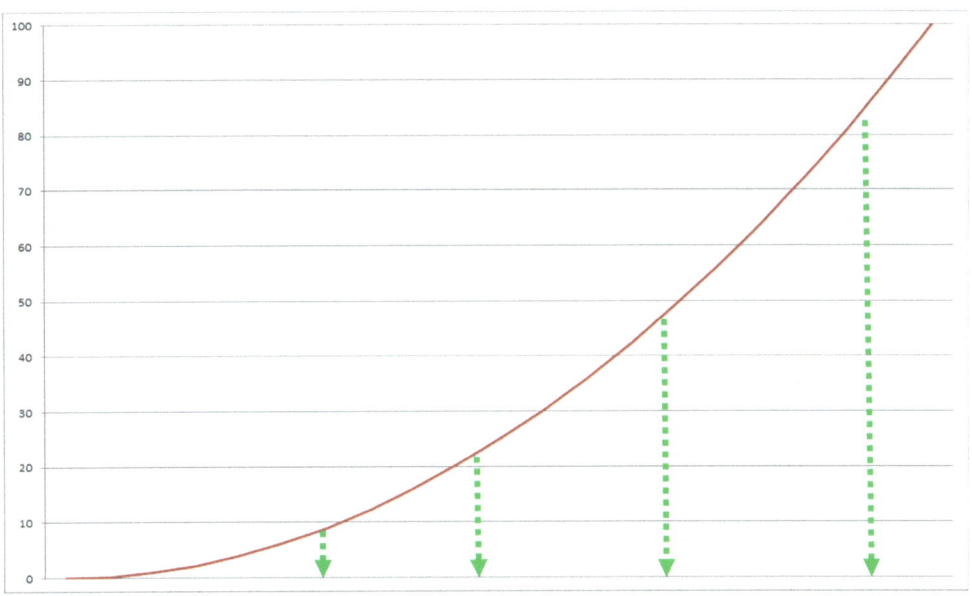

**Scenario 1**
No attempt to meet the requirements

**Scenario 2**
Some ad-hoc activities but not planned or co-ordinated.

**Scenario 3**
Beginning of planning and co-ordination. Activities started.

**Scenario 4.**
Active pursuit of the programme and visible commitment

**Scenario 5**
Programme near completion or completed. Active monitoring of performance.

65

# Index to the requirements in the Guidance Notes

**Customer Focus**

| | |
|---|---|
| Listen to customers and create a policy for satisfying their needs and expectations on delivery, price and quality, | 7 |
| Display or otherwise communicate the policy to all staff. | 9 |
| Accurately describe the product or service offered in any advertising material or catalogues. | 9 |
| Understand and agree the customer requirements with the customer before work commences. | 9 |
| Accept only those orders where the customer requirements an be met in full. | 10 |
| Include everything that significantly influences the price in any quotations given. | 11 |
| Check before delivery of product or during delivery of service that it matches the original requirements. | 11 |
| Inform customers of problems that may cause delay or change in the service or product ordered. | 12 |
| Manage changes in requirements to the customer's satisfaction and in a way that meet the needs of the business. | 12 |
| Protect customer property from loss or damage at all times. | 13 |
| Resolve customer complaints ensuring the problem does not recur. | 13 |
| Assess customer satisfaction on a regular basis. | 14 |

**Management Actions**

| | |
|---|---|
| Ensure there is clear sense of purpose and direction. | 15 |
| Set appropriate quality standards for the product or service. | 15 |
| Ensure that all employees have the skills, knowledge and necessary information to perform their tasks. | 16 |
| Provide resources so the demand for products and services can be met. | 17 |
| Provide a safe and suitable work place. | 17 |

| | |
|---|---|
| Select specialist suppliers for their capability to meet requirements. | 18 |
| Monitor specialist suppliers for their performance and impact on the quality of the business' product or service. | 19 |
| Encourage employees to share their ideas for improvement. | 19 |
| Locate, understand and fulfill legal requirements that relate to the business and its product or service. | 19 |
| Conduct Business Reviews. | 20 |

**Processes**

| | |
|---|---|
| Identify the key processes needed to produce the business' product or service. | 23 |
| Describe how these processes work together. | 23 |
| Describe the sequence of activities within these key processes. | 24 |
| Check at regular intervals that the agreed quality standards are being maintained. | 24 |
| Define roles and responsibilities. | 27 |
| Determine what documents and records need to be kept to minimize exposure to risk. | 28 |
| Determine what records need to be kept enabling performance to be checked and improvements identified. | 28 |
| Remove the potential for error and eliminate the recurrence of problems. | 29 |
| Check at regular intervals that work is consistently completed in the described way. | 30 |
| Manage changes to the processes in a controlled manner. | 30 |

www.ingramcontent.com/pod-product-compliance
Lightning Source LLC
Chambersburg PA
CBHW050745180526
45159CB00003B/1349